D1250547

Meet **Desert**
ANIMALS

Pebble®
Plus

SCORPIONS

by Rose Davin

ST. JOHN THE BAPTIST PARISH LIBRARY
2920 NEW HIGHWAY 51
LAPLACE, LOUISIANA 70068

CAPSTONE PRESS
a capstone imprint

Pebble Plus is published by Capstone Press,
1710 Roe Crest Drive, North Mankato, Minnesota 56003
www.mycapstone.com

Copyright © 2017 by Capstone Press, a Capstone imprint. All rights reserved. No part
of this publication may be reproduced in whole or in part, or stored in a retrieval system,
or transmitted in any form or by any means, electronic, mechanical, photocopying,
recording, or otherwise, without written permission of the publisher.

Library of Congress Cataloging-in-Publication Data
Names: Davin, Rose, author.
Title: Scorpions / by Rose Davin.
Description: North Mankato, Minnesota : Capstone Press, a Capstone imprint, [2017] |
Series: Pebble plus. Meet desert animals | Audience: Ages 4–8. | Audience: K to grade 3.
    | Includes bibliographical references and index.
Identifiers: LCCN 2016035498 | ISBN 9781515746010 (library binding) | ISBN
    9781515746089 (pbk.) | ISBN 9781515746263 (eBook PDF)
Subjects: LCSH: Scorpions—Juvenile literature.
Classification: LCC QL458.7 .D38 2017 | DDC 595.4/6—dc23
LC record available at https://lccn.loc.gov/2016035498

Editorial Credits
Marysa Storm and Alesha Sullivan, editors; Kayla Rossow, designer;
Ruth Smith, media researcher; Kathy McColley, production specialist

Photo Credits
Alamy: © Nature Picture Library, 13; Capstone Press: 6; naturepl.com: Angelo Gandolfi,
21; Shutterstock: Againstar, 17, Asian Images, 2, 24, Audrey Snider-Bell, 11, Charly
Morlock, 1, Dennis W. Donohue, 9, 24, EcoPrint, 7, IanRedding, 5, Mikhail Egorov, cover,
back cover, optionm, 22; TopFoto: © Photoshot, 15; Visuals Unlimited: Fabio Pupin, 19

Note to Parents and Teachers

The Meet Desert Animals set supports national curriculum standards for science
related to life science and ecosystems. This book describes and illustrates scorpions.
The images support early readers in understanding the text. The repetition of words
and phrases helps early readers learn new words. This book also introduces early
readers to subject-specific vocabulary words, which are defined in the Glossary
section. Early readers may need assistance to read some words and to use the Table of
Contents, Glossary, Read More, Internet Sites, Critical Thinking Using the Common
Core, and Index sections of the book.

Printed and bound in China.
007872

TABLE OF CONTENTS

DESERT HUNTERS

At night scorpions creep out of their burrows. They sit quietly in the darkness until prey comes near. Then they grab their prey. Sting! It's a mouse for dinner!

scorpion in its burrow

Scorpions live on every continent except

Antarctica. Many live in deserts.

But some scorpions live in grasslands or forests.

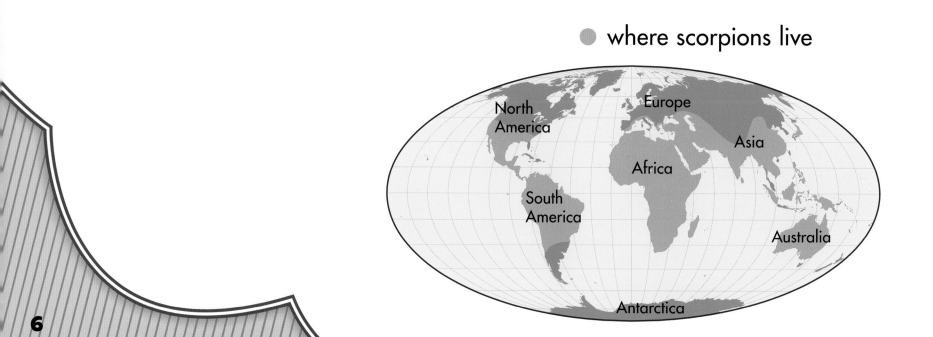

● where scorpions live

North
America

Europe

Asia

Africa

South
America

Australia

Antarctica

6

PINCERS AND STINGERS

Desert scorpions are usually black, brown,

or yellow. Most are about 3 inches (8 cm) long.

Some can be more than 7 inches (18 cm) long.

Scorpions are arachnids.

They have eight legs. Scorpions have

front pincers that are like claws.

They have stingers at the end of their tails.

stinger

pincer

leg

11

TIME TO EAT

Hungry scorpions grab prey when it comes close. They hold small prey with their pincers. Then they start eating.

Large, wiggling animals are harder
to eat. Scorpions raise their tail stinger.
Zap! The venom in the stinger
makes the animal unable to move.
It can also kill the animal.

LIFE CYCLE

Female scorpions give birth to 25

or more live young. They are all white.

Newborns climb on their mothers' backs.

Newborns live on food already in their bodies. Later mothers kill prey for their young and leave it near them. Young scorpions stay near their mothers for two or three years.

Owls, lizards, and snakes eat scorpions. Scorpions use their stingers to attack predators. Scorpions that stay safe can live about five years in the wild.

St. John the Baptist Parish Library
2920 Highway 51
LaPlace, LA 70068

21

Glossary

arachnid—a small animal that has eight legs and two body sections; scorpions and spiders are arachnids

burrow—a tunnel or hole in the ground made or used by an animal

continent—one of Earth's seven large land masses

creep—to move very slowly and quietly

desert—an area of dry land with few plants; deserts receive very little rain

pincer—a body part that is like a claw; scorpions use their pincers to catch prey

predator—an animal that hunts other animals for food

prey—an animal hunted by another animal for food

stinger—a long, sharp hollow body part; poison flows through the stinger into the prey

venom—poison in an animal's stinger used to harm or kill another animal

Read More

Marsico, Katie. *Scorpion.* Creepy Crawly Critters. Ann Arbor, Mich.: Cherry Lake Publishing, 2016.

Porter, Esther. *Scorpions.* Creepy Crawlers. North Mankato, Minn.: Capstone Press, 2014.

Shea, Therese. *Scorpions.* Things That Sting. New York: Gareth Stevens Publishing, 2016.

Internet Sites

FactHound offers a safe, fun way to find Internet sites related to this book. All of the sites on FactHound have been researched by our staff.

Here's all you do:

Visit *www.facthound.com*

Type in this code: 9781515746010

Check out projects, games and lots more at
www.capstonekids.com

Critical Thinking Using the Common Core

1. What body parts help scorpions get food? (Key Ideas and Details)

2. Why do you think scorpions stay close to their mothers for two or three years? (Integration of Knowledge and Ideas)

Index